The Guinea Pig ABC

Th

Guinea Pig ABC
by Kate Duke

A PUFFIN UNICORN

Unicorn is a registered trademark of Dutton Children's Books.

Library of Congress number 83-1410
ISBN 0-14-054756-8

Published in the United States by Dutton Children's Books,
a division of Penguin Books USA Inc.
375 Hudson Street, New York, N.Y. 10014

Editor: Ann Durell   Designer: Claire Counihan

Printed in Hong Kong by South China Printing Co.
First Unicorn Edition 1986   W
10 9 8 7 6 5 4

Awake

Bouncy

Clean

Dirty

Empty

Ferocious

Greedy

High

Itchy

Juicy

Kind

Loud

Mean

Neat

Open

Prickly

Quiet

Rich

Slippery

Timid

Upside-down

Vain

Wobbly

eXtra

Young

Zzzzzzzzz